DAD

I WANT TO HEAR ABOUT

YOUR

LIFE

Contents

Your Story Starts Here   4

Roots and Wings   7

The Boy You Were   19

First Light of Learning   29

Becoming Your Own Man   39

Love's First Whisper   53

When I Became Your Father   63

Building Our Home   71

Leisure & Passions   79

Lessons Hard Earned   91

From My Heart to Yours   99

Your Story Starts Here

You know those moments at family dinners or backyard barbecues when someone says, "Hey Dad, remember when..." - and suddenly everyone leans in closer? Like that time your first car broke down in the middle of nowhere, or that summer job that taught you more about life. Somehow, the best tales always pop up when no one's expecting them.

That's exactly what this book is for. Because let's face it - between fixing things in the garage and giving out those perfectly-timed pieces of dad wisdom, there's so much that deserves to be remembered. Not the newspaper-worthy kind, but the real ones. The ones about that nerve-wracking first date with Mom, the career decision that paid off (or didn't), and all those moments that made you the dad you are today.

Each section here might spark a memory or two. Some memories might make everyone laugh, others might raise a few eyebrows - but that's what makes them good.

Think of these pages like those conversations that happen naturally in the garage. No fancy stuff needed - just those real-life experiences that somehow taught you everything worth knowing.

The best part? There's no rush here. These pages aren't going anywhere. Maybe something comes to mind during that morning coffee or during those quiet evening moments when memories tend to surface on their own.

Because here's the thing about dad moments - they're not just stories. They're life lessons wrapped in entertainment, wisdom disguised as "back in my day" moments. And whether they're about failures or surprising wins, they're worth keeping around for the long haul.

So grab that favorite chair and let those memories roll.

Time to share your life adventures, Dad!

How to Use This Book

Throughout this book, you'll find thought-starters and memory prompts beneath each question. These are simply suggestions to spark ideas and memories - feel free to use them as inspiration or take your story in completely different directions. There are no right or wrong ways to share your life stories here. Just enjoy looking back on the path that led you here.

Dad, I've seen your smile in old photographs,

Heard echoes of your youth in your laugh,

But there's so much more I want to know -

The dreams you chased, the seeds you sowed,

The life you lived before my path.

1

Roots and Wings

Every family tree has its own rhythm of seasons. Your story begins here, in the soil of those who came before. What shaped the ground you grew from?

The First Seeds

Through the mists of time, our family story begins with those who came before you. Their courage, dreams, and determination flow through our veins. Share with us the tales of our ancestors that have been passed down to you.

Think about the stories passed down about our ancestors - their hopes, dreams, and struggles.

Tell us about your earliest known ancestors and their origins? Think about:

• The country they came from

• Their occupations

What do you know about our family name and its history?

• The origin of our surname

• Different spellings or variations

What traditions have been preserved from our ancestors? Think about:

• Cultural practices

• Special celebrations

Ancestral Land

"The land is the only thing in the world worth working for, worth fighting for, worth dying for, because it's the only thing that lasts." –
Gerald O'Hara

Picture the landscapes that cradled our family's earliest memories. What were the sights and feelings of the places our ancestors called home?

What was life like in the places our ancestors lived? Paint a picture of:

• The landscape

• How people made their living

Which places held special meaning for our family? Describe:

• Natural landmarks

• Family homes and properties

How have these places changed over time? Consider:

• Major historical events

• What remains today

A Place Called Home

Every street corner and every familiar face helped shape your early years. The community that surrounded you as you grew holds countless stories waiting to be shared. Tell us about the place you called home.

Remember the community that surrounded you growing up - the streets, the neighbors, the daily rhythms. What made this place special?

What was daily life like in your childhood community? Share:

• The pace of life

• Neighborhood routines

Can you describe how the community changed as you grew up? Tell us about:

• New developments

• Businesses that came and went

What made this place unique? Recall:

• Secret spots kids loved

• Distinctive features

The Old House

Standing at the front door of my childhood home, I can still hear the creaking of that third step and smell...

Close your eyes and walk through each room of your childhood home. What memories spring to life? What sounds echo through those halls?

What are your most vivid memories of your childhood home? Paint a picture of:

• The front entrance

• Family gathering spots

Which spaces held special meaning? Describe:

• Your favorite hideouts

• Places of comfort

What elements of home life do you remember most clearly?

• Morning routines

• Evening activities

Family Tree Tales

"To forget one's ancestors is to be a brook without a source, a tree without a root." - Chinese Proverb

Consider the characters who filled the branches of our family tree. Which ancestor's story has always fascinated you? What legacy did they leave that still influences us today?

Which ancestor's story has left the strongest impression?

• Their characteristics

• Achievements celebrated

What family legends have been passed down? Share details of:

• Historical moments

• Family heroes

How did these stories shape our family identity?

• Family mottos

• Ongoing inspiration

Grandfather's Hands

Grandfather's hands told stories that his words never could. They were maps of his life. Share with us the lessons and memories that live on through the touch and teachings of your father.

Think about your father's hands - their strength, their work, their gestures. What did those hands build, fix, or create? What lessons did they teach without words?

What skills did your father teach you?

• Work techniques

• Special talents

How did he show his care and guidance? Think about:

• Special moments

• Ways of support

What aspects of his character do you see in yourself? Consider:

• Beliefs and values

• Approaches to life

Grandmother's Kitchen

The heart of our home beat strongest in grandmother's kitchen, where love was measured in pinches and handfuls. Tell us about the aromas and wisdom that filled her kitchen.

Recall the aromas, tastes, and wisdom shared in your mother's kitchen. What life lessons were served alongside those memorable meals? What traditions still nourish our family today?

How did your mother make the kitchen come alive? Describe:

• Kitchen atmosphere

• Memorable aromas

What life wisdom did she share in the kitchen? Remember:

• Personal conversations

• Teaching moments

Which traditions from her kitchen continue today? Tell us about:

• Special occasions

• Kitchen rules

Family Portraits

Behind every familiar face in our old photographs lies a story waiting to be told. Each relative who crossed your path left footprints in your journey. Share with us the characters who colored your world and influenced your path through life.

Remember the faces that watched over your childhood - the stern uncles, the laughing aunts, the wise elders. How did each one contribute to who you became?

Who were the relatives that shaped your early years?

• Roles in family life

• Special bonds formed

What unforgettable moments did you share? Recall:

• Shared adventures

• Touching moments

How did these relationships influence who you became?

• Skills learned

• Wisdom gained

Bonds of Cousins

Summer holidays meant cousin time, when our house would over-flow with laughter and mischief. Tell us about growing up alongside your extended family.

Think about those childhood adventures with cousins - the shared secrets, the holiday gatherings, the unbreakable bonds. What memories stand out as defining moments of family connection?

What adventures did you share with your extended family?

• Holiday gatherings

• Summer activities

How did cousin relationships enrich your childhood? Think about:

• Shared secrets

• Learning from each other

What makes these relationships special today?

• Understanding without words

• Modern connections

Recipe Box

More than just ingredients and instructions, our family recipes carry stories of love, celebration, and tradition. Share with us the special recipes that taste like home and history.

Remember the dishes that brought our family together – the ones that appeared at every gathering. What stories and memories are folded into these recipes? What makes them special?

Which aromas instantly transport you back in time?

- Holiday favorites

- Comfort food favorites

Share the stories behind cherished recipes:

- The unusual ingredient

- Why some recipes remained "secret"

What makes these dishes irreplaceable?

- The hands that crafted them

- Memories they hold

Hidden Treasures

Among our family's possessions, there are certain items that hold more than their physical worth. Tell us about the family heirlooms that matter most.

Think about those special objects passed down through our family - the ones that might seem ordinary to others but hold deep meaning for us.

What stories do your family heirlooms tell?

· Where they came from

· Who owned them before

Beyond monetary value, what makes these items precious?

· Moments they witnessed

· Hands they passed through

How do these treasures connect generations?

· History they preserve

· Bonds they strengthen

2

The Boy You Were

Before you were Dad, you were just a boy with scraped knees and pocket treasures. Let's walk back to those days when the world was both smaller and somehow larger...

First Light

Memory's earliest dawn holds fragments of moments that sparkle like morning dew - perhaps a sound, a feeling, or a fleeting image that marked your first connection to the world. Share with us your earliest recollection of life's adventure.

Search through the misty corners of your earliest memories. What first clear moment emerges?

What comes alive in Dad's earliest memories?

• Favorite sounds

• Daily scenes

Paint us a picture of that time:

• Colors that stayed vivid

• Special objects remembered

Tell us about the world back then:

• Common sights now gone

• Childhood wonder

Little Adventures

Freedom had a different meaning in those childhood days. With nothing but time and imagination, Tell us about the games and adventures that filled your childhood days.

Think back to those endless childhood days filled with imagination and discovery. What games did you create? Where did your adventures take you?

Where did imagination lead you?

- Secret hideouts

- Backyard kingdoms

What games filled endless summer days?

- Creating new worlds

- Finding hidden treasures

Who joined these childhood quests?

- Loyal pets

- childhood companions

Best Friends Forever

There were friends who made childhood feel like an endless summer.
Share with us the stories of the friends who colored your early years.

Remember those childhood friendships that shaped your early years.
Who were your closest companions? What adventures did you share?
What made these friendships special?

• Shared secrets

• Adventures together

Remember those neighborhood characters:

• The daredevil

• The peacemaker

Which moments stand frozen in time?

• Standing up for each other

• Learning life lessons

School Days

Classroom walls hold echoes of lessons learned, friendships forged, and dreams sparked by inspiring teachers. Tell us about the moments that made your school days memorable.

Revisit your school years – the classrooms, the teachers, the lessons learned both in and out of books. Which moments stand out as turning points in your education?

What stands out from your early school years? Think about:

· The teacher who changed your life

· School traditions you loved

Tell us about your proudest school moments:

· That project you worked so hard on

· Awards or recognition received

What made learning come alive for you? Remember:

· Classes that sparked your curiosity

· Subjects that challenged your mind

Childhood Dreams

Every child has that magical moment when they first imagine their future. Share with us the dreams that filled your young imagination and how they shaped your path.

Think back to your childhood aspirations and imagination. What did you dream of becoming? How did these early dreams shape your path? What inspired these ambitions?

What did you imagine your future would be? Share:

• Heroes you wanted to emulate

• Places you dreamed of exploring

How did these dreams shape your choices? Consider:

• Steps taken toward your goals

• Unexpected paths that opened

Which childhood passions still influence you? Reflect on:

• Interests that never faded

• Creative sparks still burning

Getting in Trouble

Behind every childhood mishap lies a story of curiosity and valuable lessons learned. Tell us about your memorable misadventures and what they taught you.

Recall those moments of childhood mischief and their consequences. What adventures led to important life lessons?

What was the most creative excuse you ever came up with when you got caught doing something you shouldn't?

• How you thought it up

• Your parents' reaction

What's the most expensive thing you accidentally broke or damaged?

• How it happened

• Facing the consequences

What was the most valuable lesson you learned from getting in trouble as a kid?

• How it changed you

• What you tell your kids now

Childhood Heroes

"A hero is someone who has given his or her life to something bigger than oneself." - Joseph Campbell

Remember those people who seemed larger than life during your childhood years. Who did you admire? What qualities drew you to them? What impact did they have?

Who inspired wonder in your young heart? Share memories of:

• Characters from books

• Local heroes in your community

What qualities drew you to these people? Think about:

• How they handled challenges

• Special skills they possessed

Looking back now, what do you understand differently about these heroes?

• Values they modeled

• Lessons that grew clearer with time

Simple Joys

In those days before technology filled our lives, joy came in simpler packages. Tell us about the simple pleasures that made your young world magical.

Think about the toys, games, and entertainments that brought you happiness. What simple pleasures made your days special? What activities captured your imagination?

Let's explore the treasures of childhood. Remember:

• Games played for hours

• Collections carefully gathered

Paint us a picture of entertainment back then:

• Sports equipment

• Handmade fun

How did these simple pleasures shape your world?

• Friendships formed

• Joy found in little things

Family Roles

Every family is like a small universe. Your position among siblings, or as an only child, helped define your early understanding of responsibility. Share with us your role in the family dynamic and how it shaped who you became.

Consider your place in the family dynamic during childhood. What responsibilities did you have? How did being the oldest/youngest/middle child shape you?

Where did you fit in the family tapestry? Tell us about:

• Your place among siblings

• Roles that changed over time

Describe the unwritten rules and expectations:

• Tasks assigned to each child

• How conflicts were resolved

What insights do you carry forward from these early roles?

• Understanding of family dynamics

• Wisdom gained about relationships

3

First Light of Learning

School bells, chalk dust, and the weight of books under your arm. These were the days when the world began opening its pages to you. What sparked your curiosity? Who lit the way?

First Day

That morning when you stepped into your first classroom marked the beginning of a new chapter. Share with us the story of that significant first step into school life.

Take yourself back to that first day of school - the mix of excitement and nervousness, new faces and unfamiliar halls. What details stand out most vividly in your memory?

What's your most vivid memory of getting ready for your very first day of school?

• What you wore

• Who took you

Describe the moment that transformed your first-day jitters into excitement - what helped you feel like you belonged?"

• Who was involved

• Where it happened

What was the one thing about your first day that was completely different from what you'd imagined?

• Your expectations

• The reality

Favorite Teacher

"A teacher affects eternity; he can never tell where his influence stops." – Henry Adams

Think about that special teacher who went beyond just teaching subjects. What made them different? How did they inspire or challenge you? What lasting impact did they have?

Who was your favorite teacher? Tell us about:

• Grade/subject

• When did you meet

What made this teacher special?

• Their unique teaching style

• How they helped you

What would you tell this teacher today?

• Thank you messages

• Life updates

Subject of Interest

There was something magical about walking into that particular class. Share with us the academic interests that captured your imagination.

Remember when certain subjects came alive for you in school. What topics sparked your curiosity? Which classes made you lean forward in your seat?

Which subject lit up your imagination? Describe:

• Initial spark

• Favorite lessons

What class challenged you most? Share about:

• Learning hurdles

• Breakthrough moments

Which subject surprised you? Remember:

• Unexpected interests

• Eye-opening projects

After School

When the regular school day ended, another kind of education began. Tell us about the activities that enriched your school experience.

Reflect on the activities that filled your hours after the last bell rang. What pursuits captured your energy? How did these shape your interests?

What happened after the last bell?

- Exit routes

- First stops

Who did you meet after classes ended? Think about:

- Regular companions

- Meeting spots

What was your after-school routine? Describe:

- Regular paths

- Daily habits

School Friends

Friendship in school had its own special chemistry. There were those people who made even ordinary school days feel extraordinary...Tell us about the classmates who made school years special.

Think about the friendships forged in classroom moments and hallway conversations. What bonds were built during these years?

Who colored your school days? Remember:

• Close friends

• Daily companions

What adventures did you share? Think about:

• Break times

• Shared secrets

Which friendships shaped those years? Recall:

• Special connections

• Growing together

Proud Moments

Every achievement builds stepping stones of confidence. These moments of triumph, big or small, helped shape your sense of self-worth and possibility. Share with us your proudest school accomplishments.

Remember those achievements that made you stand taller. What accomplishments brought you satisfaction? Which moments of recognition meant the most?

What accomplishment from your school years initially seemed impossible but you managed to achieve anyway?"

• The challenge

• The breakthrough moment

Tell us about a time when you surprised everyone with what you could do.

• Your motivation

• People's reactions

What project or performance from your school days still makes you smile when you think about it?

• The preparation

• The final result

Learning Style

"Everyone is a genius. But if you judge a fish by its ability to climb a tree, it will live its whole life believing that it is stupid." - Albert Einstein

Reflect on how you discovered your unique way of understanding and mastering new concepts. What approaches worked for you?

How did you crack the learning code? Consider:

• Personal ways

• Working methods

Which study methods fit you best? Think about:

• Special techniques

• Learning breakthroughs

How did you overcome learning blocks? Think about:

• Solution moments

• Growth strategies

Beyond Books

Think about the practical wisdom gained during school years. What life skills emerged from your education? How did school prepare you for the real world?

What real-world wisdom did school life teach? Think about:

• Problem-solving

• Stress handling

Which skills proved surprisingly valuable? Remember:

• Networking abilities

• Negotiation skills

What everyday skills started in school? Think about:

• Goal setting

• Self-discipline

Dreams Sparked

Sometimes the smallest moments in school can shape our entire future. Tell us how your school years influenced your dreams and career aspirations.

Consider how your school experiences influenced your future path. What discoveries or experiences planted seeds for your later life? What aspirations took root during these years?

Which school experiences shaped your path? Recall:

• Club activities

• Creative projects

Who influenced your career thinking? Think about:

• Peer influences

• Role models

How did these dreams evolve? Remember:

• Practical experiences

• Skill developments

4

Becoming Your Own Man

There comes a moment when a boy first feels the pull toward his own path. Those pivotal years shaped the man you'd become. What called you forward?

Coming of Age

Every boy walks through an invisible doorway to manhood - sometimes in quiet moments of responsibility, other times through significant challenges or triumphs. Tell us about the moment you first felt yourself becoming a man.

Think back to that pivotal moment when childhood began to fade and adult responsibilities emerged. What experience marked this transition?

What responsibility or decision first made you feel like you were no longer just 'someone's son' but your own man?

• The situation

• How you handled it

Which experiences shaped your understanding of manhood?

• Role models

• Life lessons

How did your view of being a man evolve? Remember:

• Growth moments

• Responsibility growth

First Solo Flight

Independence arrives like dawn - gradually at first, then suddenly illuminating everything. Share with us your first experience of true independence.

Remember that first taste of true independence - making decisions entirely on your own. What challenges did you face? How did this freedom change you?

When did you first taste real independence? Think about:

• Solo adventures

• Freedom milestones

What emotions colored these first steps? Remember:

• Initial fears

• Excitement rushes

How did independence change your worldview? Consider:

• Life lessons

• Self-discovery

Breaking Away

"To be yourself in a world that is constantly trying to make you something else is the greatest accomplishment." - Ralph Waldo Emerson

Reflect on those moments when you chose your own path, perhaps different from family expectations. What gave you the courage? How did you balance tradition with personal growth?

What was your biggest decision that went against family wishes?

• The choice made

• Family reaction

How did you handle the pressure during this time?

• Coping methods

• Key conversations

Looking back, what did this decision teach you?

• Growth gained

• Family bonds

Finding Direction

The path to finding one's calling isn't always straight. Share with us how you discovered your vocational purpose.

Think about how your career path emerged. Was it a sudden revelation or a gradual discovery? What influences helped shape your professional journey?

What guided you toward your career path? Share about:

• Early signs of your calling

• Opportunities that appeared

Tell us about the exploration process:

• Different paths considered

• Decisions that proved pivotal

How did your direction become clear?

• Success that confirmed choices

• Vision that kept you moving forward

Inner Compass

Learning to trust your own instincts is a gradual process. This self-trust becomes a foundation for life's important decisions. Tell us about learning to rely on your own wisdom and intuition.

Consider the experiences that taught you to trust your own judgment. What situations tested your decision-making? How did you learn to listen to your intuition?

When did you learn to trust your own judgment? Remember:

• Decisions that proved right

• Times intuition guided you well

What helped develop your decision-making skills?

• Learning from consequences

• Balancing head and heart

Share how your inner guidance evolved:

• Learning from experience

• Building trust in yourself

First Job

That first employment experience taught valuable lessons about work, worth, and personal capability. Share with us the story of your first job and its impact.

Recall your entry into the working world. What surprises did you encounter? What lasting lessons came from this first experience?

What was the most surprising lesson you learned from your first real paycheck?

· Initial expectations

· How you spent it

Tell us about your most memorable mistake at your first job – and how you recovered from it.

· What happened

· How you fixed it

What skills or habits from your first job have stayed with you throughout your career?

· Daily routines

· Problem-solving

Making My Mark

Success often comes after countless small steps forward. Tell us about your first significant career accomplishments.

Think about your early career achievements. What goals did you set? What victory made you feel established in your field?

Share those breakthrough career moments:

• First major project success

• Recognition from leadership

What went into these accomplishments?

• Overcoming obstacles

• Support gathered

How did these successes shape your path?

• Confidence gained

• Networks expanded

Professional Battles

Every career path has its obstacles - challenges that test resolve, skills, and character. Share with us the career challenges you faced and overcame.

Remember those career challenges that tested your resolve. What difficulties seemed insurmountable at the time? How did you persist? What did these struggles teach you?

What challenges tested your professional mettle?

• Resource limitations solved

• Competition faced

How did you handle crucial moments?

• Strategic pivots made

• Conflicts resolved

What wisdom emerged from these battles?

• Strategies that proved effective

• Lessons about persistence

Mentors' Wisdom

Some people enter our lives briefly but leave lasting impressions. Tell us about the mentors who helped mold your growth and understanding.

Think about those who guided your professional growth. What key lessons did they share? How did their influence shape your approach?

Tell us about a mentor who saw potential in you that you didn't see in yourself - how did they help you recognize it?

• Their approach

• Key conversation

What's the best piece of career advice you received that proved invaluable over time?

• The situation

• Why it matters now

What was the toughest feedback you ever received from a mentor, and how did it change your path?

• Their message

• The transformation

Personal Code

Over time, we all develop our own set of principles. Share with us the principles you chose to live by and why.

Consider the principles that became your life's guideposts. How did you determine what values mattered most? What experiences helped form your personal ethics?

What principles became your foundation? Tell us about:

• Non-negotiable values

• Ethics in action

How did you develop these guidelines?

• Lessons from experience

• Principles tested

What helps maintain your principles?

• Daily practices

• Regular reflection

Character Tests

Sometimes life presents us with clear choices between right and wrong. Tell us about times when your principles were tested and how you responded.

Remember those moments when your integrity was tested. What situations forced you to choose between easy and right?

Share moments when integrity was challenged:

• Ethical dilemmas faced

• Pressure to compromise

How did you navigate these challenges?

• Decision-making process

• Support sought

What emerged from these tests?

• Strength discovered

• Relationships affected

Power of No

Sometimes the most powerful word we can say is "no." Tell us about learning to set limits and make tough choices that honored your principles.

Reflect on learning to set boundaries and make difficult decisions. When did you realize the strength in refusing?

Tell us about a time when saying 'no' to an opportunity actually opened the door to something better.

• The decision

• Unexpected outcomes

What was the hardest 'no' you've ever had to give to someone you cared about, and why was it necessary?

• Your struggle

• The conversation

Tell us about learning to say 'no' at work – what situation taught you the importance of professional boundaries?

• Setting limits

• Career impact

Taking Risks

Life's most rewarding moments often lie just beyond our comfort zone – in those spaces where courage meets opportunity. Tell us about the bold moves that shaped your path and the wisdom gained from taking chances.

Think about times when you stepped out of your comfort zone. What calculated risks did you take? How did you evaluate and face uncertainty?

Tell us about a risk you took that others thought was crazy, but you knew in your gut was right – how did it play out?

- Others' reactions

- The outcome

What's the biggest professional leap you've taken that could have failed spectacularly – what made you jump anyway?

- The opportunity

- Your preparation

Tell us about a risk that didn't pay off as planned – what valuable lessons did it teach you?

- What went wrong

- Recovery process

5

Love's First Whisper

Before the title of 'Dad' was yours, there was that first flutter of the heart, that spark that would eventually light a family's flame. Share the story of love's beginning...

First Crush

Young hearts learn their first lessons about love in unexpected ways.
Tell us about your early experiences with matters of the heart.

Think back to those innocent first feelings of attraction. How did young love feel? What memories stand out from those early romantic experiences?

Tell us about your most memorable attempt to impress your first crush - did it go as planned?

• Your strategy

• What happened

What's the most embarrassing misunderstanding or awkward moment you had with an early crush?

• The situation

• Others' reactions

What wisdom about love and attraction did you gain from your early romantic interests?

• Initial beliefs

• Changed perspectives

Meeting Mom

Some encounters change the course of our lives forever – like that magical moment when you first met the woman who would become your children's mother. Share with us the story of how you met our mother.

Remember that seemingly ordinary moment that changed everything – when you first saw her. What caught your attention? What made this encounter different from all others?

What first caught your attention about mom?

• First sight

• Your thoughts

How did you work up the courage to talk?

• First words

• Her response

When did you know she was "the one"?

• Key moment

• Inner feeling

The First Date

First dates are full of possibilities and nervous energy. Tell us about your first date with Mom.

Recall the anticipation and nerves of that first date. What plans did you make? What went right or wrong? How did you know this was different?

How did you ask mom out?

- The planning

- Her reaction

Where did you take her?

- The location

- The atmosphere

What conversations stood out?

- Topics shared

- Laugh moments

Love Letters

Before texts and emails, we had our own ways of showing care. One particular message I sent your mother...

Think about those special ways you communicated your growing feelings. What words or gestures expressed your emotions? How did you share your heart?

Sharing your hearts (before texting took over):

· Handwritten notes you saved

· Words you still remember

Creative ways you stayed connected:

· Surprise messages at work/school

· Little gifts with special meaning

Did you keep any messages from her?

· Special notes

· Precious words

Growing Together

Consider how your relationship developed and deepened. What experiences brought you closer? What challenges strengthened your bond?

What was your first serious disagreement?

• The issue

• Resolution found

What hobbies or interests did you develop together?

• New activities

• Shared passions

When did "I" become "we" in decisions?

• Key choices

• Compromise learned

The Proposal

Remember the planning and emotion of asking that life-changing question. What led to this moment? How did you know it was time? What made it special?

What signs told you it was time to propose?

· Inner knowing

· Clear certainty

What's the untold story of planning the proposal - from choosing the ring to rehearsing your words? Any funny moments?

· Secret prep

· Practice sessions

What happened in those first moments after "yes"?

· Her response

· Your feelings

Wedding Day

Wedding days are filled with big moments and tiny details. Tell us about the special moments and memories from the day you and Mom became husband and wife.

Reflect on the joy and significance of your wedding day. What moments stand out most clearly? What emotions filled that special day?

Morning preparations:

• Weather that day

• Pre-ceremony jitters

Moments that stand out:

• Things that went wrong but didn't matter

• Unexpected touching moments

Reception memories:

• Toasts and speeches

• How late you stayed

Early Days

Beginning a marriage is like starting a grand adventure together.
Share with us your memories of building early married life.

Think about those first years building a life together. What challenges did you face? What dreams did you share? How did you create your home?

What surprised you most about married life in those first months?

• Daily changes

• New routines

How did you both handle your first big challenge together?

• Found solutions

• Growing closer

What traditions or habits started in your first year?

• Special dates

• Unique customs

Learning Love

Marriage teaches us new definitions of love - moving beyond romance to deeper understanding, sacrifice, and partnership. Tell us how marriage changed your understanding of love and partnership.

Consider how marriage deepened your understanding of love. What did partnership teach you? How did marriage change your perspective on relationships?

What new sides of love did marriage reveal to you?

• Beyond romance

• Deep growth

How did you learn to navigate disagreements together?

• Finding balance

• Better ways

Which of mom's qualities made you love her more over time?

• Daily beauty

• Growing appreciation

6

When I Became Your Father

Nothing quite prepares you for that moment – when a tiny hand first grips your finger, and suddenly the world shifts on its axis. Everything changes, yet everything finally makes sense...

The News

Learning you're going to be a father changes everything – bringing waves of joy, responsibility, and anticipation for a new chapter in life. Tell us about when you first learned you were going to become a father.

Think back to the moment you learned you would become a father. What emotions flooded through you? How did this news change your world?

First reactions:

• Initial emotions

• Immediate thoughts

Preparation period:

• Nursery setup

• Life adjustments

What went through your mind when you first heard?

• New responsibilities

• Life changes ahead

First Hello

> *Some moments transcend words - like the first time a father meets his child. That initial connection, when eyes meet and hearts expand beyond imagination, marks the beginning of life's relationship. Tell us about the moment you first met your child and became the father.*

Recall that profound moment when you first met your child. What sensations and emotions overwhelmed you? What details remain vivid in your memory?

That life-changing moment:

• Their first cry

• Mom's glowing face

Can you describe those first few minutes?

• Their tiny grip on your finger

• Words you tried to say

When did it truly hit you that you were now "Dad"?

• Reality moment

• Life roles

New Eyes

Becoming a father changes not just responsibilities, but perspective – suddenly the world looks different, priorities shift, and life takes on new meaning. Share how becoming my father transformed your view of life.

Consider how becoming a father changed your perspective on life. What shifted in your worldview? How did fatherhood transform your priorities?

What part of your own personality did you start seeing differently once you became a father?

• Changed habits

• New priorities

Tell us about a life value or belief that completely transformed after having a child.

• Before perspective

• The shift

How did your definition of success change after having me?

• Life goals

• True meaning

First Steps

The early days of parenthood are filled with both wonder and challenge - learning to interpret cries, celebrating small milestones, and growing into the role of father. Tell us about your early journey as my father.

Think about those early days of learning to be a father. What challenges surprised you? What joys emerged? What lessons came quickly or slowly?

What was your biggest parenting surprise?

· The first time they smiled at you

· Your sudden expertise in baby language

Which moments tested your patience most?

· 3 AM feeding adventures

· Decoding why they were crying

Remember your proudest early victory?

· Getting them to sleep in record time

· Mastering the one-handed bottle prep

Dear Child

Every parent carries dreams for their child – hopes that reach beyond the present into imagined futures full of possibility and potential. Share the hopes and dreams you held for me as your child.

Reflect on the hopes and dreams you held for your child. What future did you envision? What wishes filled your heart? What promises did you make?

What dreams did you have when holding me as a baby?

• Imagining future conversations

• Wondering about their personality

Which values did you most want to pass on?

• Family traditions to continue

• Character traits to nurture

How did you envision our relationship growing?

• Being their protector

• Sharing special moments

Father's Prayers

Every parent carries silent prayers for their children. Share with us the prayers and wishes you've held for me through the years.

Think about your deepest wishes and concerns for your child's future. What prayers filled your quiet moments? What hopes pressed on your heart?

What was your deepest wish for me during nighttime moments?

- Future thoughts

- Love wishes

When did you most strongly feel the need to protect me?

- During my first illness

- Seeing me vulnerable

What did you silently pray for most often?

- Strength to guide me well

- Courage for my journey

Daily Joys

Parenthood's greatest treasures often lie in ordinary moments - bed-time stories, shared laughter, small discoveries, and quiet conversations. Tell us about the special moments you've cherished in everyday parenting.

Recall those special moments in everyday parenting. What small delights surprised you? What simple moments became treasured memories?

What's the most entertaining or heartwarming conversation we had during an ordinary car ride?

• The setting

• Why it stuck

Describe a moment when my simple question or observation made you see something familiar in a completely new way.

• The context

• Your realization

What made you laugh the most during everyday routines?

• My creative excuses

• Mealtime adventures

7

Building Our Home

More than walls and windows, you built a world for us. Each decision, every sacrifice, was another brick in the foundation of our family's story. What vision guided your hands?

First Keys

Few moments match the significance of receiving keys to your first home. This milestone marks the start of creating a family's physical foundation. Tell us about purchasing your first home and what it meant to you.

Remember the milestone of purchasing your first home. What emotions filled that moment? How did it feel to create your own space?

How did you know this house was "the one" when you first saw it?

• Gut speak

• Heart click

What sacrifices did you and mom make to save for this home?

• Budget tight

• Time wait

What's your most vivid memory of our first night in this house?

• Take-out dinner

• Floor sleep

Dream Space

Creating a family home involves more than just furnishing rooms – it's about crafting spaces that nurture, comfort, and inspire those who live there. Share how you worked to create the perfect environment for our family.

Think about creating the perfect environment for your family. What vision guided you? How did you make this space uniquely yours?

Which room transformation are you most proud of and why?

• Vision accomplished

Family collaborated

What were your biggest hopes when creating each of our childhood bedrooms?

• Dreams encouraged

• Personal touches added

Tell us about your favorite spot in our home – what makes it special and how did it become that way?

• The location

• Shared moments

Family Rituals

Houses become homes through the rhythms of daily life - morning routines, evening traditions, and special practices that give structure to family living. Tell us about the special routines that made our house truly feel like home.

Consider the routines and traditions that made your house feel like home. What daily practices brought comfort? What rituals united the family?

What mealtime ritual or tradition do you think brought our family closest together?

• How it started

• Special moments

Describe a weekend tradition that seemed ordinary at the time but now holds special significance in your memory.

• Regular activity

• Shared moments

What unique family tradition did you intentionally create, hoping it would stick - did it work out as planned?

• Your vision

• Family response

Gathering Place

A home grows warmer with each gathering it hosts. Share how our home became a center for bringing people together.

Reflect on how your home became a center for friends and family. What made it welcoming? How did you create this atmosphere?

What made our home welcoming to others?

• Comfort features

• Warm welcomes

Which gathering stands out most in memory?

• Celebration moments

• Family gatherings

What unexpected challenges or joys did you discover in making our home a welcoming space for others?

• Surprises

• Rich rewards

Growing Garden

"A garden is a grand teacher. It teaches patience and careful watch-fulness; it teaches industry and thrift; above all it teaches entire trust." - Gertrude Jekyll

Think about nurturing your outdoor space. What satisfaction came from watching things grow?

What inspired you to start our family garden, and how did it grow beyond your initial vision?

• Dreams carefully planted

Family involvement

Which garden element brought the most satisfaction?

• Growing success

• Harvest moments

What's your most memorable garden project we worked on together?

• First tomato patch

• Tools side by side

Memory Corners

Every home develops its sacred spaces over time. Share the meaningful places in our home and the memories they hold.

Remember those special spots in your home that hold particular meaning. What stories do these spaces tell? What memories do they hold?

Which spot holds the most cherished memories?

• Comfort places

• Special events

What made certain areas extra meaningful?

• Personal touches

• Shared activities

How did these special places evolve over time?

• Added meanings

• Deeper connections

Family Table

Our family table witnessed countless moments of connection. Tell us about the special moments that happened around our family table.

Consider the role of shared meals in building family bonds. What conversations unfolded here? What memories were made?

What conversations shaped our family culture?

• Daily sharing

• Laughter moments

Which mealtime tradition meant the most?

• Special recipes

• Holiday customs

How did shared meals strengthen our bonds?

• Communication growth

• Together time

8

Leisure & Passions

Beyond the daily duties and responsibilities, there were those moments that made your spirit soar – hobbies that refreshed you, interests that sparked joy. What captured your heart in those free moments?

Weekend Warrior

Weekends were your time to pursue what you loved most. Tell us about the activities and hobbies that brought you joy during your free time.

Think about those activities that helped you recharge and find joy outside of work. What weekend pursuits brought you the most satisfaction? How did these activities balance your life?

What weekend activity made you feel most alive and renewed?

• Pure joy

• True passion

How did your weekend interests evolve through different life stages?

• Time changes

• New interests

Remember the most epic weekend adventure?

• That unexpected discovery

• Our greatest achievement

Sports & Games

Competition and physical activity build more than just strength. These athletic pursuits shape both body and character. Tell us about your involvement in sports and competitive activities.

Consider your relationship with sports and competition. What games drew you in? What athletic pursuits challenged you?

Which sports do you like best and why?

• Initial attraction

• Growing passion

Which athlete or team has inspired you most, and how did their story impact you?

• The choice

• Lasting influence

What sports moment you witnessed (live or on TV) left the strongest impression, and why?

• The event

• Lasting memory

Collector's Corner

Collections tell stories about what we value – each item gathered holding personal meaning or memory. Share with us what you've collected over the years and the stories behind these treasures.

Think about the items you've collected over time. What sparked these collections? What stories do they tell? What makes each piece special?

Tell us about how your first collection started and what drew you to these particular items.

• First piece

• Growing interest

Which item in your collection holds the most surprising or unexpected story?

• The piece

• Special value

How did your collecting interests evolve over the years?

• Taste change

• New paths

Nature Calls

The outdoors beckons with promise of adventure, peace, and connection to something larger than ourselves. Tell us about your outdoor adventures and what they've meant to you.

Reflect on your experiences in the outdoors. What adventures called to you? How did nature refresh your spirit? What discoveries did you make?

Which outdoor memory stands out most vividly?

• Star-gazing nights

• Animal encounters

What natural place became your favorite sanctuary?

• Peace spot

• Heart home

How did nature teach you its most powerful lesson?

• Wild wisdom

• Life truth

Self-Taught

Learning something new takes patience and persistence. Share with us the skills you've developed through your own initiative and interest.

Consider the skills you pursued on your own. What motivated you to learn? How did you teach yourself? What challenges did you overcome?

What skill did you most enjoy teaching yourself from scratch?

• Learn joy

• Mind grow

Which self-taught ability surprised others the most?

• Hidden skill

• Show moment

What self-taught skill has proven most valuable in unexpected ways?

• Learning process

• Surprise uses

Workshop Tales

Creation brings satisfaction - whether building, fixing, or crafting something with our own hands. Tell us about the things you've made and the stories behind them.

Think about the projects you've created with your own hands. What inspired these creations? What challenges did you face? What achievements brought pride?

What's the most meaningful thing you've built or fixed for someone else?

- The project

- Shared joy

Which project pushed your skills to new levels, and how did you overcome its challenges?

- Skill stretch

- Breaking through

Tell us about a creation that started small but grew into something much bigger.

- First idea

- Evolution

Reading List

Remember the books that influenced your life. What stories captured your imagination? What knowledge shaped your thinking? What authors spoke to you?

Which book changed the way you see the world?

• Mind shift

• View change

Which author seemed to speak directly to your heart?

• Voice match

• Soul speak

What book helped you through a challenging time?

• Life guide

• Heart heal

Musical Notes

Music has always been a part of life's important moments. Tell us about your relationship with music and the songs that have meant the most to you.

Consider your connection to music over the years. What songs marked important moments? How did music move you? What melodies still resonate?

Which song instantly takes you back to a special moment?

- Soul song

- Memory tune

Which musician or band has influenced your life the most, and why do they stand out?

- First discovery

- Special sound

Share a musical tradition or favorite song you've passed down to your kids.

- The choice

- Why special

Movie nights

Movies have always been more than just entertainment – they're windows into different worlds, mirrors of our own experiences, and timekeepers of our memories.

Remember the movies that influenced your life. What stories on screen captured your imagination? What characters spoke to your soul?

Which movie do you wish you could watch again for the first time, and why?

• The film

• Magic elements

Share a film that you and Mom both love – what makes it special for you both?

• First watch

• Still treasure

What movie villain actually made you think differently about life?

• The character

• Changed view

Adventure Partners

Some interests are best shared – having companions who share our passions makes activities more enjoyable and meaningful. Tell us about the special people who've shared your interests and adventures.

Reflect on those special people who shared your interests and adventures. What made these partnerships meaningful? How did they enhance your experiences?

Who influenced your interests most significantly?

• Lifelong friends

• Inspiring figures

What's the most memorable misadventure you've had with a friend that you laugh about now?

• The plan

• What happened

Share a story about an unexpected adventure with a friend that brought you closer.

• Surprise moment

• Shared challenge

Future Projects

Dreams of future activities keep us moving forward - plans and aspirations for new adventures and creative pursuits. Share with us your plans for future hobbies and activities.

Consider the dreams and plans still waiting to be realized. What projects call to you? What new skills beckon? What adventures remain?

What's a skill or hobby you've always wanted to try but haven't yet - and what draws you to it?

- The interest

- Future vision

What's a place or activity you're saving for retirement, and why does it excite you?

- The plan

- Looking forward

Share a creative project you've been thinking about but haven't started yet.

- Inspiration

- Planning thoughts

9

Lessons Hard Earned

Life writes its story in both shadow and light. Through challenges and triumphs, you navigated our family's ship. What anchored you during storms? What stars guided you home?

Inner Strength

Facing difficulties requires finding reserves of courage we might not know we had - drawing on faith, determination, and resilience to move forward. Share how you found the strength to face life's challenges.

Think about discovering your own resilience. Where did you find strength? What helped you persevere? How did you maintain hope?

What's the hardest lesson life taught you that you're now grateful for?

• Tough time

• Wisdom gained

Tell us about a time when patience and persistence finally paid off.

• The goal

• Staying strong

What did you want us to learn from watching you push through?

• Silent resilience

• Steady persistence

Silver Linings

Even in life's storms, unexpected blessings can emerge – lessons learned, relationships strengthened, or new directions discovered. Share the unexpected good that came from difficult times in your life.

Remember those unexpected gifts found within difficulties. What surprising good emerged? What positive changes resulted? What appreciation grew?

Share a time when a 'closed door' opened a window you hadn't noticed before.

- Lost chance

- New opportunity

Which surprise blessing had the biggest impact?

- Family bonds

- True friendships

How did finding silver linings change your outlook?

- Hope in darkness

- Gratitude grown

Relationship Rules

Understanding people and building meaningful connections requires wisdom gained through experience. Share what you've learned about building and maintaining relationships throughout your life.

Think about what you've learned about human connections. What insights about relationships proved true? What principles guided your interactions?

What taught you most about maintaining connections?

• Listening well

• Trust built

Which relationship principle proved most valuable?

• Silent support

• Honest words

How did fatherhood change your view of relationships?

• Deeper patience

• Stronger bonds

Health Choices

Wellbeing encompasses body, mind, and spirit - lessons about maintaining health often come through personal experience and observation. Tell us about the important health lessons you've learned and what you wish you'd known earlier.

Consider the lessons learned about maintaining wellbeing. What health wisdom proved most valuable? What choices made the biggest impact?

When did health become a priority for you?

- Energy needs

- Future thoughts

What's a health habit you wish you'd started much earlier in life?

- Past routine

- Current benefit

Tell us about something you learned about mental well-being that changed your life.

- Key insight

- New approach

Time's Value

Time becomes more precious as we age. Share how your under-standing of time's value has evolved and what you've learned about spending it wisely.

Remember how your understanding of time's importance evolved. What taught you about using time wisely? What priorities emerged?

What made you realize time was your real wealth?

• Kids growing fast

• Moments missed

Which time investment gave the best returns?

• Family dinners

• Shared hobbies

How did fatherhood change your use of time?

• Quality focus

• Present living

Success Defined

Success means something different to everyone, and that meaning often changes. Share how your understanding of true success has changed over time and what you now believe it means.

Consider how your definition of success has changed. What shaped this evolution? How has your perspective shifted? What truly matters?

How did becoming a dad change your view of success?

• Impact meaning

• Family first

What success matters most now?

• Life balance

• Value living

When did your definition of winning change?

• Parent perspective

• Life purpose

Living Well

A well-lived life means different things to different people. Tell us about your philosophy of life and what you believe makes life good and meaningful.

Reflect on your philosophy about what makes a good life. What principles guide you? What values proved most important?

Looking back at all life's ups and downs, what would you tell your younger self makes a truly good life?

• Quiet strength

• Daily kindness

After raising kids and seeing life's full picture, how has your view of "living well" changed?

• More presence

• Deeper listening

As a father who's weathered many storms, what daily choices have proven most worthwhile?

• Morning hugs

• Dinner talks

10

From My Heart to Yours

Some words wait a lifetime to be spoken. They rest quietly in a father's heart. Now is the moment to share these treasured thoughts and these prayers that have been whispered countless times...

Dear Child

My dearest child, there are some things a father's heart holds so deep that words seem inadequate...

Write from your heart about your deepest love and hopes for your child. What dreams do you hold? What feelings often go unspoken? What wishes fill your heart?

When I watch you sleep at night or see you tackle life's challenges, here's what fills my heart:

• Silent pride

• Endless hope

Through all the homework help and driving lessons, here's what I've seen grow in you:

• Kind heart

• Bright spirit

After all our shared laughs and tears, here's what I dream for your journey ahead:

• Rich peace

• Deep joy

If I Could Tell You

Some truths ripen slowly in our hearts - important things we wish we'd expressed earlier but needed time to fully understand. Here are the things I've wanted you to know.

Consider those important truths you wish you'd shared earlier. What wisdom seems more urgent now? What feelings need expression? What understanding wants sharing?

Between the rushed mornings and busy evenings, here's what I wish I'd said more often:

• Proud always

• Here forever

Through all the sports games and school plays, here's what I hoped you saw in me:

• Never quitting

• Keep learning

When life gets tough and I'm not around, here's what I want echoing in your heart:

• Home's waiting

• You're enough

Values Passed Down

Certain principles form the cornerstone of a life well-lived. These are the fundamental truths I hope will guide your path as they've guided mine. Here are the values I most want to pass on to you.

Consider the core principles that guided your life. What values proved most essential? Which principles weathered life's tests? What truths do you most want to transmit?

When your kids watch you handle life's challenges, which principles do you hope shine through?

• Truth matters

• Work honors

Through daily choices and quiet moments, what legacy are you building step by step?

• Integrity lasts

• Courage grows

Between spoken lessons and lived example, what values matter most to pass on?

• Choose kind

• Stay strong

Dreams Forward

*Every parent carries dreams that stretch beyond their own lifetime –
hopes that bloom in future generations and continue growing through
time. Let me share the visions I hold for our family's tomorrow.*

Consider your hopes for future generations. What dreams do you
hold for those to come? What future do you envision?

What legacy do you most hope to pass down through generations?
• Values deeply rooted

• Stories carefully preserved

What wisdom do you hope your grandchildren will carry forward?
• Character traits valued

• Dreams courageously pursued

Which family traditions do you hope will continue through generations?
• Gatherings kept alive

• Values staying strong

Time Capsule

Life holds special milestones ahead - moments I may or may not share with you, but want to be present for in spirit. These messages are meant for specific future moments in your life journey. Open them when you reach these milestones.

Create messages for specific future moments in your child's life. What wisdom will they need? What support should they remember?

For your wedding day:

• Choose partnership

• Keep growing together

For becoming a parent:

• Time moves faster now

• Joy outweighs worry

For major life transitions:

• Change brings growth

• Roots give wings

My Prayer

The deepest wishes of a parent's heart often take the form of prayer - hopes lifted up for protection, guidance, and blessing over a child's life. Here is what I pray for your life.

Express your deepest hopes and wishes for your loved ones. What blessings do you seek? What protection do you pray for?

What prayers do you say for us most often?

• Nighttime reflections

Future paths blessed

Beyond nightly bedtime prayers, what deepest hopes rise from a father's heart?

• Health staying strong

• Peace surrounding us

Through all life's twists and turns ahead, what blessings do you wish most?

• Strong wings

• Brave spirit

Mom's Edition Now Available

Mom, I Want to Hear About Your Life

Every mother holds precious memories waiting to be shared. Through thoughtfully crafted chapters like "Childhood Dreams," "Love's Journey," and "A Mother's Heart," this beautiful book creates space for mothers to share their life experiences, cherished memories, and gathered wisdom.

The perfect companion to "Dad, I Want to Hear About Your Life," this book helps capture your mother's remarkable journey - from her early adventures to her deepest hopes for her children. Each page invites meaningful conversations and preserves precious memories that might otherwise go untold.

Give the gift of storytelling. Help your mother share her life's journey.

Available at major online bookstores:

- Amazon

- Barnes & Noble

- and other leading online retailers

www.ingramcontent.com/pod-product-compliance
Lightning Source LLC
Chambersburg PA
CBHW051324120626
46547CB00015B/2378